GONE FISHING WITH SAMY ROSENSTOCK

TOADHOUSE, a.k.a. Allan Graham, was born in San Francisco, California, in 1943. He is an artist whose work includes sculpture, painting, poetry, and video.

SNUGGLY BOOKS

THIS IS A SNUGGLY BOOK

Copyright © 2016 by Allan Graham
All rights reserved.

Edited and compiled by Brendan Connell.

ISBN: 978-1-943813-10-0

Front cover art by Allan Graham.

The back cover shows Toadhouse, a.k.a. Allan Graham,
in his studio (photo by Gloria Graham).

toadhouse

GONE FISHING WITH SAMY ROSENSTOCK

the stairs led by each
to the following place
the surface contributed
to the distance—but
by and by opportunity
was past

What comes out is more complex than what comes in.
(Description is more complex than experience.)

We often say more than we know.

Meaning = Interpretation
Memory is the expansion of experience.
Thought is information. Reality is a word!

Cerebral snare.
Cranial projection → fabric for rent.

Language is a hairy hand.

RIVER CROSSING = 14ft
MEANINGLESSNESS = 15ft
Waving outside the window @ 25ft
NO WORDS EXPRESS = 16ft

MOVE
MORE
LESS
ZERO
PUSH
SKIN
BOTH
SCAL(E)
HAVE
MUCH
BODY
SELF
TODA(Y)
ALIE(N)
OTHE(R)
BEIN(G)
LOOK
LAFF
DEBT
LEAP
FALL

the cup was being filled
satisfaction was close
at hand the cup valued
its use and through it
knew the intimacy of lips
in a way we can only envy

squatting behind a bush
the lord of the manor
never realized that all
he left behind would
contribute to equality
with time . . . . .

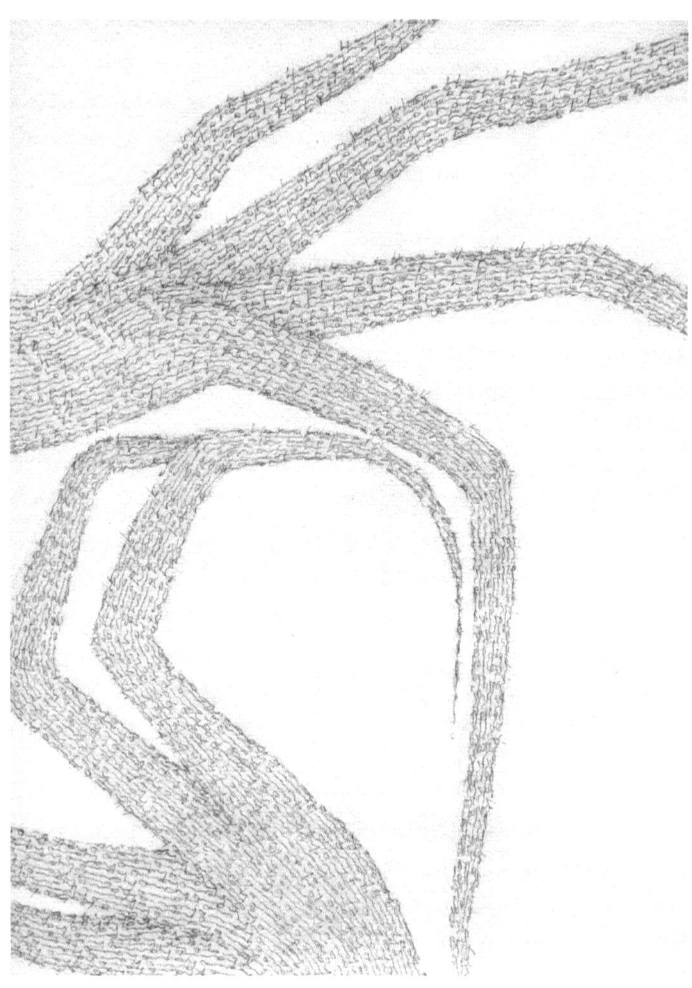

(A) FIELD GUIDE

TO THE FIELD
TO ~~NO~~ PLACE
TO EFFORTLESSNESS
TO REGARDLESS
TO FALLING
TO A NOTEBOOK
TO UNDERSTANDING
TO UNDERESTIMATING
TO REDUNDANCY
TO ENTROPY
TO FOLLOWING
TO MASS PRODUCTION
TO MASS DISTINCTION
TO CLEAN THOUGHT
TO A BOOK COVER
TO COLLECTING DUST
TO OTHER THINGS
TO SHRINK WRAP
TO HAPLESSNESS
TO EASY DIEING
TO EVERYWHERE
TO THOUGHT
TO ERROR

TO STUDY
TO STUPIDITY
TO MOVING YOUR HEAD
TO NEANDERTHALISM
TO RETALIATIONISM
TO OPENMINDEDNESS
TO FOOTPATHS
TO RETALIATIONISM
TO DETAILS
TO ESCAPISM
TO DUST(MITES)
TO LIMITED THINKING
TO TEMPORALITY
TO (THE) OBVIOUS
TO THINNESS
TO COMMONALITY
TO ABSURDITIES
TO MISINFORMATION
~~TO PERFECT THOUGHT~~
TO THOUGHT CORRECTION
TO LIMITED ADDITION
TO LIMPING SLIGHTLY
TO INDIFFERENCE
TO SMALL OBJECTIONS
TO ~~BOWEL~~ MOVEMENT
TO BROKEN PROMISES
TO CONSENSUAL THOUGHT
TO CERTAIN LIMITATIONS
TO CONSTIPATION

the world was created
from gas and dust
from ideas and souls
from changeless
changed
the incomprehensible
compromised

DEAD
STILL?

SHIT IN
A STATE OF
DENIAL—
OUT LIVING A
THOUGHT

WATCHING
A HAND
BASKET GO
TO HELL

LIFE IS
A SCARE
TACTIC

they were told that
the light they saw was dead
dead for millions of years
their eyes perceive only
the past—all that is seen
has already been—this
stopped them in their tracks

CONSCIOUSNESS:
A LIFE SUSPENSION
SYSTEM
EARTH MOVES
AROUND THE
SUN~
WHAT A
DRAG

HOW
THERE
THEM !

LIFE—
A SEASONED
PREMIER

LINGUISTIC
SENSATIONS . . .
IN RED
SAUCE

THE GREAT
END
RETURNS!

MEMORY
DOES NOT
FUNCTION
WITH A
FULL
DECK

LIFE?
SOMEBODY
HAS TO DO IT . . .

FRIENDS
FOR A
GAY
TOMORROW

HALF DEAD
AND STUPID
YOUR VOTE
COUNTS—
THEME PARK
RECALL !

"HUMAN
INTELLIGENCE"
(NOW THERE
IS AN IDEA)
LIFE'S
A SHUFFLE
LIFE'S
A DEAL

TEMPORALITY :
THE ULTIMATE
ANARCHY

FOOT
IN
MOUTH
DISEASE

PANDORA'S BOX—
A PORNOGRAPHIC
PEEK INTO
HUMANOID
FUTURES

LIPS
STICK

TWO
 DEBATE ONENESS
(DEAD HEAT)

WITHOUT
TIME
WHERE WOULD
WE BE ?
GOING
WHERE EVERYONE
HAS GONE
BEFORE

NOW
IS A
LOCATION !

NO TIME
LIKE THE
PRESCIENT

FEEDING
HABITS OF
THE
WAYWORD
MIND

HAMMER
BLOWS
DISTANCE

there is no sense to the
beauty of it nor the
terror of ignorance and
the disquieting love that
moves the body beyond
comprehension

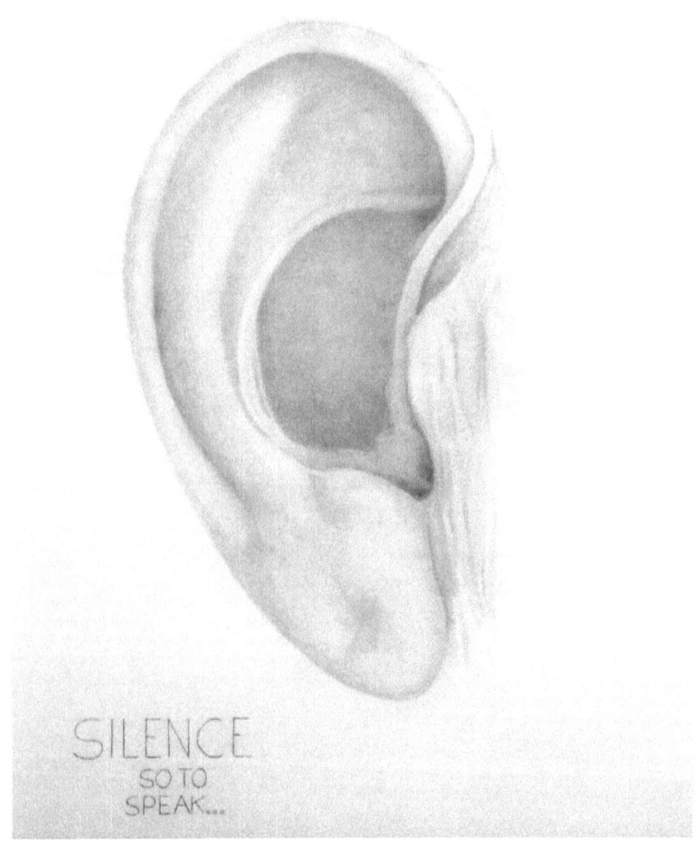

Carl Rakosi's ear

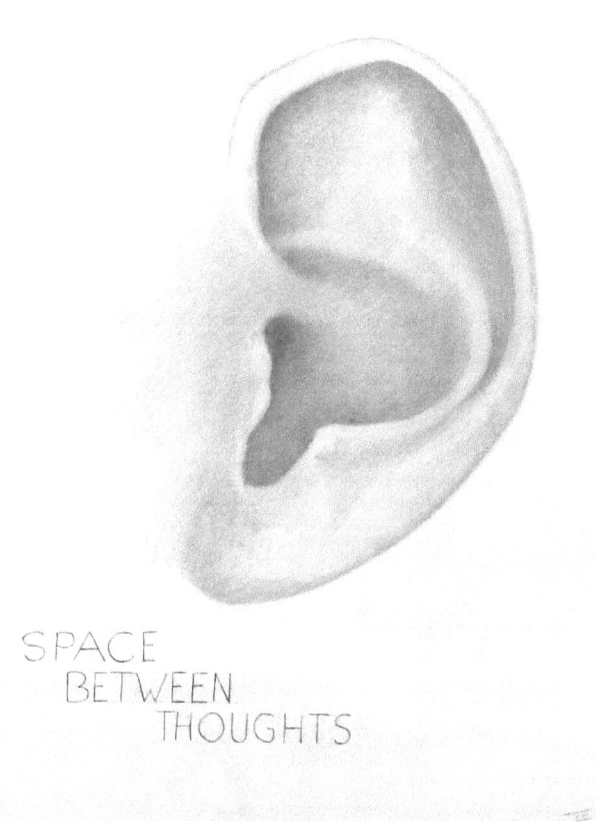

Philip Whalen's ear

cognitive ambrosia
a heedless on-going
a dilapidated profusion
diminishes with
returns . . .
(many have plundered this whole)

PURE WHEN
PURE ALWAYS
PURE THAT
PURE TIME
PURE INSTANT
PURE OUR
PURE SPACE
PURE HERE
PURE SUCH
PURE LIMIT
PURE REALITY
PURE PLAIN
PURE ONLY
PURE WHILE
PURE IDEA
PURE CHOICE
PURE IS
PURE THING
PURE AS
PURE TWO

it leads—the path
to places seen constantly
yet over and again refused
as notice—for notice
requires as we take—so
much so that most of us
are not willing to give

SOME THINGS
are so absurd
that I will not write them
down—but friend the older
I get the more I believe that
—absurdity is the staff of life—
ask a round if you can find
one.

(ADULTERY)
where does reality
lie &
with
whom?

THE
MIRROR
THOUGHT
OF
YOU

(just a reflection)

on the front porch
lay a feather
it lay there very still
the wind had not found it
the porch didn't mind
the feather was light
and stillness
served it's purpose

EAR TO MOUTH

the distance between the mouth
and the ear is different for each person—
an example—for some it is infinite &
for a few it doesn't exist—though the distance
between ear & mouth is often short——
. . . . for a few it is thoughtful . . . .

A
N
Y
P
O
S
I
T
I
O
N
L
I
M
I
T
S
T
H
E
V
I
E
W

most of you probably don't believe
in Aliens—that is other life forms—
other than what we accept as "real" or
from another space—*outer or inner*
another world etc.
whether you believe in Alien habitation
here on earth or not—Sunday is swap
day . . . .

. . . . ***PLEASE***

I would like to voice
a complaint—there are
things within that are
missing. I don't know if they
were stolen, misplaced or just
left out from the beginning
& I am not sure to whom
I should speak.

PRESCIENT

Some believe in a full
complement far—with no host in
sight—yet
in truth it is a no host
far—with occasional
complements
. . . . of insight
so belly up—
the choices pre-date
. . . . the experience

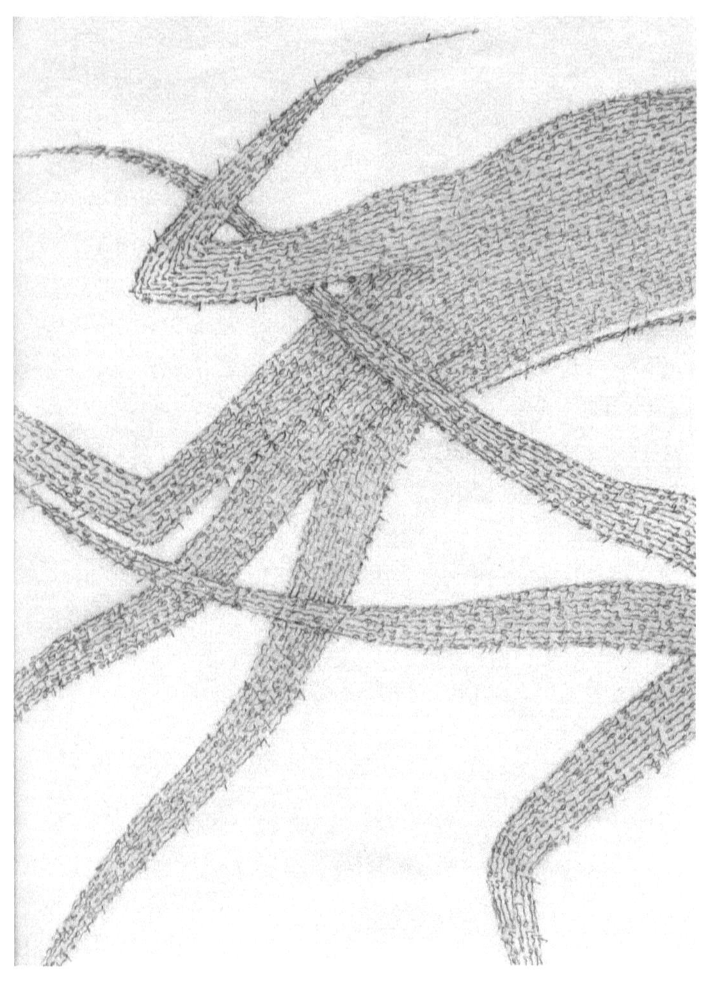

would every body please move
to the center of the bus—we are
approaching the Metaphysical
Clearing House
LAST STOP

TONGUE pursuing ***LIPS*** in a **soft** universe

ENIGMA circumventing a pair of ***1/2*** clusters

ONCE in a ***two*** system

FROM & FORM in an ***if*** shower

FISH – HILL & STREAM
in a + & – universe

TO & FROM entering an ***un***-formation

TIME engaging ***proximity***

CLICKTOENLARGE.COMA

~~THOUGHT~~
~~THOUGHT~~
~~THOUGHT~~
=
a frog
in the
throat

floating
calmly by the bank
duck leaves
deposit

the symbol kept confusing
itself with the metaphor
the trail was well worn
so it should have been easy
but that was the trouble
you see!

WE NEVER KNOW WHY FOR SURE—
OR IF THERE IS A "WHY"
OR A "FOR SURE" . . .
BUT WE NEED TO KEEP ON MOVING
OR WE SEEM "NOT TO BE"—
WHY? I AM NOT SURE.

what you have here is a something
graduated in turns—a stratified
formulation situated and balanced
on a notion

NOSE
AIR
FLOWS
KNOWS
NOT
WHY

IT
IS
ON
LOAN

reluctance accepted its own
pronouncements—tailoring input
for future generations . . .
walls were presented in
perspective

duration is a
mystery
that only the
moment can
apprehend

GROPETHERAPY.COMA

MASSDISTINCTION.COMPOST

SUNRISE––––SUNSET.CALM

CRAZY
the WAY
HEADS
APPEAR
AT
THE ENDs
OF NECKS

www.ingramcontent.com/pod-product-compliance
Ingram Content Group UK Ltd.
Pitfield, Milton Keynes, MK11 3LW, UK
UKHW042011190726
13854UKWH00005B/2242